# My Keepsake Bible

*Stories by Lizzie Ribbons*
*Illustrations by Paola Bertolini Grudina*

CONCORDIA PUBLISHING HOUSE · SAINT LOUIS

*This Bible is a gift to*

micah Christian Bailey

West Branch *from* United
Methodist Church

*On the occasion of*

your baptism!

*on this date*

January 20, 2019

*Father God, Creator of all that is good,*
*thank You for the gift of this precious child,*
*the miracle of this special baby,*
*the wonder of new life,*
*the mystery of human love,*
*and the love of Your Son, Jesus Christ.*

*See what kind of love the Father has given to us,
that we should be called children of God;
and so we are.*

*1 John 3:1*

My name is ...................................................................................................

........................................................................................................................

I was born on ............................................................................................

I weighed ...................................................................................................

My eyes are ................................................................................................

My hair is ........ ..........................................................................................

I live at this address: ...............................................................................

........................................................................................................................

........................................................................................................................

My grandfather's name

..............................................

My grandfather's date and place of birth

..............................................

..............................................

..............................................

My grandmother's name

..............................................

My grandmother's date and place of birth

..............................................

..............................................

..............................................

My father's name

..............................................

My father's date and place of birth

..............................................

..............................................

..............................................

*My grandmother's name*

.....................................................
*My grandmother's date and place of birth*

.....................................................

.....................................................

.....................................

*My grandfather's name*

.....................................................
*My grandfather's date and place of birth*

.....................................................

.....................................................

.....................................

*My mother's name*

.....................................................
*My mother's date and place of birth*

.....................................................

.....................................................

.....................................................

*My name*

.....................................................

.....................................................

.....................................

My Family

*O God, Your generous love surrounds us,*
*and everything we enjoy comes from You.*

\*

*Lord, bless us and protect us.*
*Lord, smile on us and show us Your love.*
*Lord, help us and take care of us.*
*Lord, guide us, keep us, and grant us Your peace.*

# My Progress

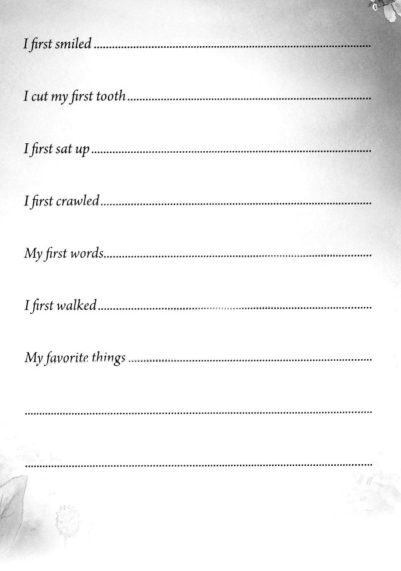

*I first smiled* ........................................................................

*I cut my first tooth* ...............................................................

*I first sat up* .........................................................................

*I first crawled* ......................................................................

*My first words* .......................................................................

*I first walked* ........................................................................

*My favorite things* ...............................................................

........................................................................

........................................................................

# Bible Stories and Prayers

### PRAYERS

# God made the world
### (Genesis 1)

Long ago, at the beginning of time, God said, "Let there be light," and bright light shone in the darkness.

God said, "Let there be land and sea," and land filled with mountains appeared, surrounded by deep water.

God said, "Let there be trees and plants, sun, moon, and stars," and the plants produced fruit in the sunshine and were cool under the moon and stars.

God said, "Let there be fish and winged creatures," and the sea swam with fish and the sky was filled with birds and butterflies.

God said, "Let there be all kinds of animals," and tigers padded and antelope galloped over the land.

God said, "Let there be people to look after My beautiful world," and there were, male and female.

God saw that His world was good, and He rested.

# Noah builds an ark

(Genesis 6:14–9:17)

God told Noah to build an ark. Soon there would be a flood that would cover the earth.

So, just like God said, Noah built an ark, a very, very big boat. When it was finished, Noah took his family and all the animals, two by two, inside.

Then it began to rain: *splish, splash, splish, splash.*

The water covered the ground, the trees, and even the mountaintops. But Noah and his family and the animals were safe inside the ark.

Days passed and nights passed before the rain stopped. One day, when a dove came back carrying an olive leaf, Noah knew that soon it would be safe for them to leave the ark.

Then God sent a beautiful rainbow. "There will never be a flood like this again," God promised.

# Under the stars

### (Genesis 12; 15)

A very long time ago, a rich man called Abraham lived in a big city called Ur.

God told Abraham to leave his house and travel from place to place until God gave him a new home in a new country.

Abraham trusted God. He took with him his wife, Sarah, and his nephew Lot. He took his servants and his sheep and his goats. Abraham and his family lived in tents as they traveled.

"Come and look at the stars," God said to Abraham one dark and twinkly night. "You are just the beginning.

"There will be many, many people in your family. There will be many, many children born to the people in your family. There will be as many in your family as there are stars in the sky."

When God said this, Abraham had no children. He and Sarah were getting old. But Abraham knew God. He knew that God always keeps His promises.

# Three visitors

(Genesis 18; 21)

One hot day, three visitors came to Abraham as he rested in the shade.

"Here's water for washing and drinking," said Abraham. "Come and rest and eat."

Sarah cooked her very best food, and Abraham served the food to the visitors as they sat under the shady trees. Sarah stayed in the tent and listened as the men talked.

"Soon Sarah will give birth to your baby son," said one of the men to Abraham.

"I'm much too old to have a baby!" Sarah laughed to herself. "I'm old enough to be a grandma!"

"Nothing is too hard for God to do," said the man. "Just wait and see."

Then Abraham knew that God had sent the men with a message for him. So they waited, and they trusted God, and soon, Sarah's baby boy was born. They called him Isaac.

# Isaac and Rebekah

## (Genesis 24)

Abraham loved his son Isaac. When Isaac was a grown-up, his father wanted to find a wife for him. Abraham sent his servant on a long journey back to his home country to find someone for Isaac to marry.

When the servant arrived in Abraham's country, he stopped at a well. The servant prayed to God to send a girl who would be kind enough to draw water for him and for his ten thirsty camels.

A beautiful young woman arrived. "Would you like some water?" she asked him. "Can I get water for your camels too?" This girl was Rebekah. God had answered the servant's prayer.

Rebekah was the granddaughter of Abraham's brother. Her family welcomed Abraham's servant and listened as he explained why he had come.

The servant took Rebekah back with him. Isaac knew that he loved her and wanted her to be his wife.

# Joseph and his brothers

(Genesis 37)

When he was grown up, Isaac had a son named Jacob. And Jacob had a son named Joseph. Jacob had eleven other sons, but he loved Joseph the most.

Jacob gave Joseph a beautiful coat to wear. "That's not fair," his eleven brothers said. They were angry because Jacob had not given them nice gifts.

One day, Joseph dreamed that the sun and the moon and the stars all bowed down to his star! He dreamed about bundles of corn that his brothers had grown. They all bowed down to Joseph's own bundles of corn. "So you think you're special?" complained his brothers. "You think we'll bow down to you like that?"

They were so angry that they threw Joseph into a deep, dark pit. Then they sold him to some traders who were going far away to Egypt. And they lied to their father, Jacob, telling him that a wild animal had killed Joseph.

But God protected Joseph. Joseph worked hard for a kind master. Then, one day, he met the king of Egypt.

# Dreams come true

(Genesis 40–45)

The king of Egypt had strange dreams. Joseph helped him
understand the dreams. "In my dreams, I saw seven thin
cows eat seven fat cows," said the king. "And I saw seven dry
ears of corn eat seven plump ears of corn."

"The dreams mean that seven years of good harvests will be followed by seven very bad years," said Joseph. "God is warning you about the future."

The king was happy with this news. He gave Joseph an important job—storing food to help the people when there was none.

Back in Canaan, Jacob's family was very hungry indeed. So Jacob sent his sons to Egypt to buy food.

Joseph remembered the horrible things his brothers had done to him, but he still loved his brothers and missed them very much. He knew that God had made everything good again.

"It's me!" said Joseph. "I'm your brother. Bring our father here too, so we can all live together in Egypt."

# The baby in the basket

(Exodus 1–2)

Long after Joseph lived and died, there were thousands
of God's people living in Egypt. The king was afraid that all
the baby boys would grow up to be men who would fight
him. The king wanted to get rid of the little boys.

One day, baby Moses was crying loudly. His mother was
very afraid that the king's soldiers would hear him. So she
put baby Moses in a basket and floated the basket on the
River Nile, where he would be safe.

Big sister Miriam hid in the bushes by the river and watched her baby brother floating about in the basket. And who should come along but the king's own daughter!

"Oh!" said the princess. "What a sweet baby. I'll take him to live with me!"

Miriam stood up. "I know someone who can help you," said Miriam. And she fetched her mother, the baby's mother, to help care for Moses.

Now everyone was happy. And God had kept baby Moses safe.

# The king who said "No!"
### (Exodus 6–12)

When Moses was a grown-up, God spoke to him from a bright, burning bush.

"Moses, you are going to lead My people out of Egypt to a better place," said God.

"But I can't! I don't know how," Moses said.

"Yes, you can," said God. "You can do anything that I ask you to do because I will help you."

The king of Egypt had made God's people his slaves.

"Let my people go," Moses said to the king of Egypt. But the king said no, and God punished him.

The rivers turned to blood. Then there were frogs and gnats and flies everywhere, hopping and buzzing.

The animals and people became ill. Huge hailstones rained down from the dark sky, and clouds of insects chomped at the crops until the ground was bare.

"Let my people go!" Moses said to the king of Egypt. But still the king said no.

Finally, after lots of people had died, the king changed his mind.

"Go, go, GO!" said the king of Egypt.

# Follow-my-leader

(Exodus 14)

Moses led God's people out of Egypt. Every day, a tall cloud showed them where to go. Every night, a tall fire showed them where to rest.

When they reached the Red Sea, Moses lifted his stick, and the wind blew a path across the sea so that everyone could cross over on dry land.

When the people were hungry, God sent food from heaven. When they were thirsty, He provided water. The people grumbled, but they followed Moses day by day, and Moses followed God day by day.

One day, Moses climbed high on a mountain and talked
with God. When he came down the mountain, he brought
with him ten special rules to help the people live together
happily. These rules are called the Commandments.

# The Commandments
### (Exodus 19–20)

"I am the one true and living God," God said. "Don't worship anyone else. Don't worship pictures or statues.

"Use My name when you talk to Me and treat My name with respect.

"Rest on the seventh day of the week—make it a special day when everyone can worship Me together.

"Obey your parents and love them always.

"Don't murder anyone.

"Don't take someone else's wife or husband and treat them as if they are your own.

"Don't steal anything that belongs to someone else.

"Don't tell lies or say nasty things about people.

"Don't look at the things other people have and want them so much that you try to get their things from them.

"Don't look at other people's family or friends and want them so much that you try to take them away."

Moses told the people, "We must love God and be kind to one another. This is how God wants us to live."

# Walls come tumbling down

(Joshua 1–6)

When Moses died, Joshua became the new leader of God's people.

"Don't be afraid, Joshua," said God. "Trust Me, and I will help you."

God was going to lead His people into a beautiful land. But first, they had to cross the River Jordan—wide and fast and deep and dangerous.

"Don't be afraid," Joshua told the people. "Trust God, and He will help us."

As the people stepped into the river, the water dried up! Everyone crossed safely to the other side.

Then they had to get past the walls of Jericho. The walls were tall and thick and wide.

"Don't be afraid," said Joshua. "Trust God, and He will help us."

Joshua's soldiers did lots of marching around the city walls. The priests did lots of blowing on trumpets. The people did lots of shouting . . . and the walls of the city came tumbling down!

Then Joshua and God's people lived in Canaan, the land God had promised them.

# Gideon's sign from God

(Judges 6)

The Midianites rode down on their camels and took all the food that God's people were growing. Gideon was hiding from them.

"Hello!" an angel said to him one day. "God wants you to help His people."

Gideon looked around him. Was the angel really talking to him?

"People have forgotten the rules God gave them," said the angel. "God wants you to help the people remember them again."

"But I am not big or clever or special, and my family is not big or clever or special. Are you sure God wants me to help?"

God did, indeed. And He proved this to Gideon. Gideon laid his dry wool on the ground, and God made it wet. Then, when the ground was wet with dew, God made Gideon's wool dry.

This was how Gideon knew that God could do anything and that God had chosen him to help His people. Gideon trusted God. And God helped them all to live in peace again.

# Ruth in the wheat field

## (Ruth)

Lots of sad, bad things had happened to Naomi, but God was kind and good. He sent Ruth to take care of her.

"Lots of sad, bad things have happened," said Ruth, "but I will go with you to Bethlehem and look after you, and I will love God."

Ruth worked in the wheat field. God was kind and good to her. He sent Boaz to make sure she had enough food to take home to Naomi.

"God is kind and good!" said Naomi. "First, He sent Ruth to take care of me, and now He has sent Boaz to take care of us both!"

After a while, Boaz married Ruth. They were very happy together. They had a baby boy called Obed.

"God is kind and good!" said Naomi. "First, He gave me Ruth, and then He sent Boaz to take care of us both. Now, He has made us one big family to take care of each other!"

# The voice in the night
(1 Samuel 1–3)

Hannah wanted a baby very much.

"Please help me," Hannah prayed to God. "I do so want a baby, and any child I have will be Yours as well."

God gave Hannah and her husband a baby boy. She called him Samuel, and she was very happy. When Samuel was old enough, Hannah took him to the temple.

"I will teach him about God and the right way to live," said Eli the priest. "I will look after Samuel."

One night, Samuel woke to hear someone calling his name.

Samuel ran to old Eli.

"Here I am," said Samuel to Eli.

"I didn't call you," said Eli. "Go back to bed."

Samuel heard the voice again.

"Here I am," said Samuel again.

"I didn't call you," said Eli. "Go back to bed."

Then Samuel heard the voice again.

This time, Eli knew it was God calling Samuel.

"Tell God you're listening to Him," said Eli.

"I'm listening, God," said Samuel. "I will always listen to You."

# Seven sons and a shepherd boy

(1 Samuel 16)

When Samuel was a grown-up, he helped God's people. He always trusted God, and God helped him.

Now the people wanted a king. Samuel asked God to help him choose the right person.

Jesse brought seven of his sons to Samuel.

Should it be the tallest and strongest? thought Samuel.

One, two, three, four, five, six, seven. Jesse's sons were tall and strong.

Then God whispered in Samuel's ear. "Not the tallest, not the strongest, but the person who is good and true inside."

"Have you any other sons?" Samuel asked Jesse.

"Well, there's David," said Jesse. "But he's out in the fields taking care of the sheep."

"I'll wait for him," said Samuel.

When David came, Samuel said, "This is who God has chosen to be king. Not the tallest, not the strongest, but the person who is good and true inside."

He sprinkled drops of oil on David's head. One day, David would be king.

# David and the giant

(1 Samuel 17)

David was not as big as a soldier, but Goliath was very, very big. He was huge. He was enormous. He was a GIANT!

Goliath's army stood on one side. King Saul's army stood on the other side looking very worried.

"Who will come and fight me?" Goliath shouted day after day.

Goliath wore a lot of heavy armor. He looked mean and fierce and very bad indeed. Everyone was very afraid of him, everyone except David.

"I'll fight him," said David. "God helped me fight lions and bears when I looked after my sheep. He will help me now."

46

"What?" roared the giant. "You're just a boy!"

David found five stones in the stream. He put one in his shepherd's sling. Then he let the stone fly. Goliath fell to the ground. And that was the end of the big, bad giant.

King Saul's army cheered and shouted, and Goliath's army ran away!

# "God is my shepherd"
(Psalm 23)

David wrote a lot of songs. Some of his songs were happy, and some were sad. Some were brave, and some were bold. Some praised God, and some were prayers to Him.

David told God everything because God was his friend.

48

David knew that God was with him all the time—when he was happy, when he felt sad or frightened, even when he felt lonely or grumpy.

"God is my shepherd," David sang.

"I am His sheep.

God leads me where it's rough and steep,

or by still waters, cool and deep.

He walks beside me every day,

in all the places where I play,

in every step along the way.

I walk behind Him in his light,

in the darkness shining bright.

I know I'm always in His sight.

He spreads out food and comes to greet—

'Everybody, take a seat!

Everybody, come and eat!'"

# A very wise king
(1 Kings 2–10)

King Solomon was king of God's people.

"What would you like Me to give you?" asked God.

Solomon thought hard. Did he want to be rich and famous and have lots of money? Did he want to be strong and brave and live forever? Did he want lots of things for himself?

"I would like to be good and wise, fair and just—a good king who rules his people well."

God was very pleased with Solomon's answer. He made Solomon good and wise, fair and just, but He gave him lots of other good things too.

All sorts of people came to Solomon. He told them how to live a good and happy life.

Then King Solomon built a great and wonderful temple for God.

"This is a special place where Your people can come to ask You to forgive them and to worship You," said Solomon. "But I know that You do not live in any kind of house. You are with us, God, wherever we are."

# Elijah and the ravens

## (1 Kings 17)

"There will be no rain for a very long time," said Elijah to King Ahab. "God is angry about the bad things you have been doing. There won't be much to eat or drink. The earth will be dry and bare."

"Hmmmm," said King Ahab, who wasn't sure he believed Elijah.

God told Elijah to go and stay by a little stream where there was water. Every day, God sent ravens—large black birds—to Elijah with food in their beaks. Gradually, the water in Elijah's stream dried up.

"Go now to the little village of Zarephath," God told Elijah. "There is a widow there who will make sure you have enough to eat."

"It's all I have left," the widow told Elijah. "After this, I have no more flour or oil to make bread." But for as long as she shared her food with Elijah, God made sure she had enough flour and oil to make bread.

# Fire on the mountain

(1 Kings 18)

There was still no rain. It was time for Elijah to go back to the king.

"Let's choose between the real God and the stone statue you worship," said Elijah.

Elijah laid wood on top of a stone altar, and the people who believed Baal was god did the same.

"Come on, Baal!" shouted the people who worshiped the pretend god. "Light our fire! Listen to us and answer! Listen to us!"

They shouted until they were exhausted, and their throats were sore. But nothing happened.

"Has Baal run away?" teased Elijah. "Perhaps he's gone to sleep! Perhaps he's on vacation!"

Then Elijah poured water all over his wood. "Let everyone see that You are the one true and living God," Elijah prayed to God.

Then fire fell from heaven, and the wood sizzled and burned. The people fell to their knees and worshiped God. Then God sent rain once more to the earth.

# A dip in the river

(2 Kings 5)

A little servant girl from another country lived in the house of an important soldier named Naaman. She saw that he had spots and nasty sore places all over his skin. The girl told the soldier's wife that God could help him.

So Naaman sent a message to the king in the servant girl's country.

"What do you expect me to do?," the king said. "You could go and visit Elisha, the prophet."

So Naaman went to visit Elisha.

"Go and wash in the River Jordan seven times," said Elisha's servant.

Naaman wasn't happy. He said, "First Elisha sends his servant instead of seeing me himself. Then he tells me to take a bath! I thought he'd wave his arms or say some prayers!"

"Go on, Naaman," said his servant. "Just do what he says."

Grumpy Naaman went into the river seven times. And the spots and the blotches vanished! Naaman couldn't stop smiling. God had healed him.

# Jonah and the very big fish

(Book of Jonah)

God told Jonah to go to a city called Nineveh.

But Jonah didn't want to go. The people in Nineveh were cruel and wicked. So Jonah got on a boat and sailed away in the opposite direction.

A big storm blew, and the sailors were afraid they'd all be drowned.

"Throw me into the sea!" said Jonah. "It's all my fault! I've disobeyed God."

"If that's what you want," said the sailors, "we'll do it."

The sailors threw Jonah into the water, but a very big fish swallowed him up in one large swallow.

Jonah stayed inside the fish for three days and three nights. Jonah prayed, and he prayed.

The very big fish spat Jonah out of its mouth on to the beach. This time, Jonah did what God said. He went to the city of Nineveh and told the people there to stop doing bad things. The people listened to him! They said they were sorry, and God forgave them.

"That's why I sent you to Nineveh," said God. "Now these bad people have changed their ways. That's good!"

# The terrible fiery furnace
(Daniel 3)

Shadrach, Meshach, and Abednego were prisoners in faraway Babylon. One day, the king told everyone to bow down and worship a golden statue.

"I won't worship the statue," said Shadrach.

"I won't either," said Meshach.

"Neither will I," said Abednego.

"There will be trouble if you don't!" said the king's messenger. "As soon as you hear music, you must worship the golden statue, or you'll be thrown into the fiery furnace!"

"We will worship the one true God and no one else," they said. So Shadrach, Meshach, and Abednego were thrown into the blazing fiery furnace. It was very, very hot.

But the three faithful men did not get burned. Not one little bit! God sent His angel into the fiery furnace to keep them safe.

When the king brought them out of the fiery furnace, he knew that their God was the one true God!

# Plots and plans and lions
## (Daniel 6)

Daniel was also a prisoner in Babylon. The king liked Daniel very much, but the king's men did not. They came up with a wicked plan to get rid of Daniel.

The wicked men told the king, "Everyone should say that you're the most special person on earth. If they don't, they should be thrown to the lions."

"Yes!" said the king. "I agree!"

Then the king's men made a law that everyone should worship the king. Anyone who didn't would be thrown to the lions.

Daniel knew about the law, but he prayed only to God.

"Daniel still prays to God," they told the king.

"Daniel loves God more than you," they said.

"Daniel has broken your law," they said.

"Enough!" said the king.

The king knew he had to obey the law and throw Daniel to the lions. "I hope your God will save you," he said to Daniel.

It was a long, lonely night for the king, but in the morning, he found Daniel alive and well!

"I trusted God. I prayed to Him, and He took care of me," said Daniel.

"Your God is the one true and living God," said the king. "He is amazing, and we will all worship Him!"

# Mary meets an angel
## (Luke 1)

To most people, Mary was an ordinary girl, but God thought she was very special indeed. One day, God sent the angel Gabriel to see her.

"Don't be afraid," said the angel. "I have a message for you from God. You are going to have a baby. The baby will be God's own Son, and you are to name Him Jesus."

"But I am still young, and I don't have a husband yet," she said.

"Don't worry, Mary," Gabriel said. "Nothing is too hard for God to do."

Mary was a little afraid, but she was also very happy. She ran to tell her cousin Elizabeth the news.

"You are very special, Mary!" Elizabeth said. "Everyone will know how much God has blessed you."

Mary prayed to God. "You are wise and wonderful," she said. "I rejoice in You!"

# A long way to Bethlehem
(Luke 2)

The angel Gabriel told Joseph, a village carpenter, to marry Mary and take care of her and her baby. The baby grew inside Mary, and soon the time came for her son to be born.

The Romans wanted to count all the people in the empire. Mary and Joseph had to travel a long way to Bethlehem so they could be counted. When they reached Bethlehem, the town was very busy.

"No room here!" they were told when they looked for a place to stay. "But you can rest in the stable, if you like."

That night, Mary's baby was born. He was Jesus, the Son of God. Mary wrapped Him up and made a bed for Him in the manger where the animals ate.

This day is called Christmas.

# Some very good news!

(Luke 2)

That night, shepherds were out in the hills looking after their sheep. Suddenly, there was a bright light all around them! They heard the voice of an angel!

"Don't be afraid," said the angel. "I have good news for you! Jesus, the Son of God, has been born in Bethlehem. You'll find Him lying in a manger."

Then many more angels appeared, singing songs of praise to God.

The shepherds were excited. They ran to see the baby in the manger for themselves.

They found baby Jesus with Mary and Joseph. The shepherds told them about the message of the angels. Then they told everyone they saw what had happened that night.

# Following the star
### (Matthew 2)

After Jesus was born, there was a very bright star shining in the sky. Wise Men who lived far away saw the star and knew it was a sign from God.

"A new king has been born to the Jewish people," said one of the Wise Men.

"We must take gifts to Him," said another.

"We must go to worship Him," said another.

They made a long, long journey, following the bright star all the way until they found Jesus, the newborn King, with His mother, Mary.

They gave Him gifts of gold and frankincense and myrrh. They worshiped Him—Jesus, the Son of God.

# Jesus is lost
(Luke 2:41–51)

Every year, Jesus grew bigger and stronger. When He was
old enough, Jesus went to the temple in Jerusalem with
Mary and Joseph and many other people. They went for a
festival called Passover.

When Jesus was twelve years old, something frightening
happened for Mary and Joseph. They were on their way
home from Jerusalem when Mary realized Jesus wasn't with
them.

"Where's Jesus?" she asked.

They searched among their friends; they searched
among their family. But they couldn't find Jesus anywhere!

So Mary and Joseph hurried back to Jerusalem to see if He was there. It was three days before they found Jesus. He had been in the temple all the time, listening to the teachers.

Jesus told them, "I needed to be in God's house—My Father's house—so I could learn all about Him."

Jesus went home with Mary and Joseph. He grew taller and stronger and went on learning about God.

# An invitation to a wedding

(John 2:1–11)

Mary had been invited to a wedding. Jesus and some of His friends went too. Jesus was a grown man now. Mary knew that He had special work to do for God.

After a while, the wine ran out. There was nothing left to drink. Mary spoke to Jesus.

"Can You do something?" she asked Him. "If there is no wine, the party will be ruined."

"Fill the jars with water," Jesus said quietly to the servants. "Fill them right up to the top, and then take some to the man in charge of the feast."

"What a surprise!" said the man who tasted it. "This is wonderful wine! It's the best!"

Jesus' friends were amazed. Jesus had made the water into wine—the very best wine!

# Very special friends
(Mark 1:16–20)

Jesus had some very special friends. He wanted them to help Him tell people about God. He wanted them to be with Him when He helped bad people become good people, sad people become happy, and ill people to become well again.

The first four friends were fishermen: Peter, Andrew, James, and John. They were working beside the sea when Jesus asked them to leave their nets and follow Him.

Matthew, the tax collector, was counting his money when Jesus asked him to come with Him.

There were twelve friends altogether: Peter, Andrew, James, John, Philip, Bartholomew, Matthew, Thomas, James (yes, there were two!), Thaddaeus, Simon, and Judas. They were called "disciples."

Sometimes the disciples went out two by two, telling everyone the good news.

"God loves you!" they said.

"God wants you to love Him."

"God wants you to love other people and to be part of His special kingdom."

# The Lord's Prayer

(Luke 11:2–4)

Jesus loved God and loved to talk to Him by praying.
So He told His friends how to pray to God too.

"Don't use fancy words that don't mean much," Jesus said. "Tell God what you really feel. He wants to hear about everything that worries you. Say something like this:

"Our Father in heaven, Your name is great and holy. Help us to do things that are good and right so that everyone will know who You are and so Your love will spread all over the world.

"Please give us all we need to live each day, and help us to be kind to one another always. Keep us safe from harm and from doing wrong things.

"For You are the only true, wise, and wonderful God, and Your kingdom will last forever. Amen."

# God cares about you
(Matthew 6:25–34)

The disciples were often with Jesus when He talked to people about God.

"Don't worry too much about food and drink and clothes," said Jesus. "Look at the birds and the flowers. Our heavenly Father looks after the birds, and they all find food. And the flowers are beautiful! God has dressed them all in fine colors.

"God gives us all we need. He cares for everyone, even the tiniest sparrows," said Jesus. "God is great and mighty and powerful, and He knows about it if one falls to the ground. He knows us and cares about us too. We are safe in His world."

81

# The hole in the roof

(Mark 2:1–12)

A crowd of people had gathered in Capernaum to listen to
Jesus. Four men wanted to see Jesus too. They wanted Him
to help their friend who couldn't walk.

But it was so crowded that the friends couldn't get into the house. They couldn't see Jesus at all! So they carried their friend up to the roof.

They scraped at the roof until they made a hole. Dust flew everywhere until the hole was big enough for them to let their friend down into the house—right at Jesus' feet. Jesus was happy to meet him.

"Hello," Jesus said. "You can get up and go home now. Your sins are forgiven, and your body is healed."

"Who does Jesus think He is?" muttered some of the religious teachers who were in the room.

But others were amazed as the man picked up his mat and went home.

# The story of two houses

(Matthew 7:24–27)

Jesus told many stories to teach people about God.

"A man built a house," Jesus said in one of His stories.
"The man built it on good strong rock, which was solid
and safe.

"Another man built a house too," said Jesus. "He chose a place on the sand, where it was much easier to dig.

"One day there was a great storm. The rain rained hard. The rivers rose higher and higher. The wind whistled— whoo-oo! The first man's house stood firm and safe in the storm. But the second man's house was built on the shifting sand—and soon his house fell to the ground.

"Build your life on the true and solid rock of My Word," Jesus said, "so it won't tumble around your ears when troubles come."

# The storm at sea

(Mark 4:35–41)

It was the end of a long, tiring day. Jesus and His friends were sailing across the Sea of Galilee. It was a quiet night, and soon Jesus fell asleep.

Suddenly, a storm blew up. The wind whistled: whoo-oo, and the thunder boomed: rumble, rumble, and the waves washed into the boat: woosh, woosh.

Jesus' friends were very afraid, but Jesus stayed sound asleep.

"Wake up!" they said to Jesus. "We're going to drown! WAKE UP!"

Jesus stood up and spoke to the wind and waves. "Hush. Be quiet," said Jesus. The wind quieted, and the waves stopped sloshing. Everything was calm. And Jesus' friends were not afraid anymore.

Jesus had calmed the storm!

# A very worried father
(Luke 8:41–56)

Jairus's little girl was very sick. She lay in bed feeling hot and tired, achy and ill. She felt so sick that Jairus went to find Jesus to ask Him to help her.

That day, many people wanted to see Jesus. There were crowds of people pushing and jostling around Jesus. So it took some time for Jairus to reach Jesus, and it took some more time for Jesus to come with him.

"It's too late!" said someone from Jairus's house. "Your little girl has died!"

Jairus was very upset. But Jesus went into his house with Peter and James and John.

"Trust Me," Jesus said. Then Jairus and his wife watched as Jesus took her hand. "Wake up, little girl," Jesus said.

Jairus's daughter opened her eyes and sat up. It was a miracle!

"She's hungry," said Jesus. "Give her something to eat."

# A very big picnic
(John 6:1–14)

There were thousands of people out on the hillside to hear
Jesus talk. The people had been listening to Jesus tell them
stories about God. They saw Him make blind people see and
heal people who were sick.

By evening, everyone was hungry. Then a little boy came to Jesus with five little bread rolls and two little fish that his mother had given him for lunch. The boy shared all he had with Jesus.

"Thank You, God, for all You give us," said Jesus, giving thanks for the food.

Then the disciples handed out the food to everyone. Jesus had turned a little bit of food into enough for thousands of people. It was a very big and happy picnic. There was even food left over. It was another miracle.

# The story of the Good Samaritan
(Luke 10:25–37)

"How can I show God that I love Him?" a man asked Jesus one day.

"Love God and love other people too," Jesus replied. Then He told them another story. "A man was walking along a lonely road when he was attacked and robbed.

The man lay by the side of the road, hurting all over. He couldn't even open his eyes.

"Then he heard footsteps coming nearer, and then going away, on the other side of the road.

"Again, the man heard footsteps coming nearer, and then going away, on the other side of the road.

"Then the man heard clippetty-clop, clippetty-clop—a man on a donkey. But he was from another country. He was a stranger, an enemy!

"The stranger did not walk away as the others had. He wrapped the man's wounds, helped him onto his own donkey, and took him to an inn to get better. Although he was an enemy, the Samaritan had looked after the wounded man as if he really cared about him. You should show care to all people too," Jesus said, "even to people who are not your friends."

# The story of the lost sheep
### (Luke 15:1–7)

"God loves you like a good shepherd loves his sheep!"
Jesus once said. Then He told a story.

"Once there was a shepherd who had one hundred
sheep. But one of the sheep wandered off from the others.
It nibbled juicy grass and skipped over the hills and ran far
away.

"The little sheep wandered farther and farther. The day grew dark and cold, and there wasn't any more juicy grass— only rocky hills and prickly bushes. The little sheep was lost.

"That night, when the shepherd counted his sheep, he saw that one was missing. He left the ninety-nine other sheep and walked all over the hillsides until at last he found his little lost sheep. Then he carried the sheep safely in his arms down the rocky path toward home.

"'I'm really happy I've found you,' said the shepherd. 'Let's have a party! Let's celebrate!'"

# The story of the loving father
(Luke 15:11–32)

"God loves you," said Jesus. "God waits until you are ready
to say you have made a mistake and to say you are sorry.
God is like the father in this story.

"The father had two sons. The younger son left home,
taking his share of his father's money. The younger son was

rich! He spent his money on all sorts of things, until finally he had spent it all!

"Now he was so poor that he had to work on a pig farm. He was so hungry that he wanted to eat the pigs' food! So he decided to go home to his father.

"His father saw him coming from a long way off. He was overjoyed to see his son!

"'I'm really sorry,' said the young man to his father. 'I've been selfish and greedy and . . .'

"But his father was already calling to his servants.

"'My son has come home!' he shouted. 'Bring his best clothes, a ring for his finger, and shoes for his feet. Let's celebrate!'"

# The man who couldn't see
(Mark 10:46–52)

Bartimaeus was blind. He could smell the flowers but he couldn't see them. He could hear the wind rustling in the leaves but he couldn't see the trees. He could feel the hot sun but he couldn't see the blue sky.

Bartimaeus was blind and could not work. He sat by the roadside, day after day, begging for money.

One day Bartimaeus heard the sound of a happy crowd coming along the road. When Bartimaeus realized that Jesus was coming, he called out.

"Jesus!" called Bartimaeus. "Help me!"

"Who's there?" said Jesus.

Then kind hands helped Bartimaeus to his feet and led him to Jesus.

Jesus knew that Bartimaeus wanted to see, so He healed him. Suddenly, Bartimaeus could see the flowers and the trees and the blue sky. And he could see Jesus!

Bartimaeus thanked God. Then he followed Jesus along the road.

# Zacchaeus meets Jesus
(Luke 19:1–10)

Zacchaeus had lots of money. But he had not always been a kind man or a good man, and he had no friends. People said he was a cheater.

Zacchaeus wanted to see Jesus, but so did many other people, and Zacchaeus was too small to see over their heads. So he climbed up a fig tree and looked over the heads of all the people.

He saw Jesus walking along the road and saw Him coming closer and closer until . . . Jesus was looking up at Zacchaeus!

"Come down," said Jesus. "I'm coming to your house today."

Zacchaeus climbed down through the branches as fast as he could. He took Jesus to his house.

"You're my friend now," said Zacchaeus to Jesus. "I'll give half of my money to the poor, and I will give back money to anyone I have cheated."

Jesus said, "I have come to save people like you." And Zacchaeus was very happy to know Jesus.

# Jesus rides a donkey

(Matthew 21:1–11)

Jesus and His friends were on their way to the big city of Jerusalem.

"There's a little donkey in that village," Jesus said to His friends one day. "No one has ever sat on its back. The donkey is young and wild, but I want you to bring it to Me."

Just as they were told, Jesus' friends fetched the donkey. They put their cloaks over the donkey's back and helped Jesus climb on. Then Jesus rode the donkey into Jerusalem.

The city was noisy and exciting. Crowds of people welcomed Jesus. Many men, women, and children followed too. They put their cloaks down on the road in front of Jesus. They threw palm branches in front of Him. They cheered and waved and shouted.

"Hosanna!" everyone cried out.

"Praise God!"

"Praise the King of peace!"

"Praise King Jesus!"

# The woman who loved God
(Mark 12:41–44)

Jesus and His friends were near the temple.

People were dropping money into a box. Some rich people made sure others were looking as they put LOTS of money in the box.

Then a poor woman came along. She didn't look to see who was watching. She didn't care at all what people thought of her. She came to the temple because she loved God. Quietly, she dropped two little coins into the box.

"Look," said Jesus to His disciples, "this woman has been very generous. The rich people gave a lot of money, but they still have lots of money left. This woman is all alone in the world. She has hardly enough to eat, yet she has given all the money she has. The widow has given far more than anyone else because she loves God."

# Jesus prays in the garden
(Mark 14:12–51)

Later in the week, Jesus and His friends ate together.
Jesus was thoughtful.

He offered them bread and said it was His broken
body; He offered them wine and said it was His
blood. Jesus told them this was for the forgiveness of
sins, and He said they should remember Him.

After supper, they went to a garden, where Jesus
prayed to God. "I will do whatever You want," Jesus
prayed. "But please help Me."

Jesus knew that Judas had gone to tell
His enemies where He was so they could
arrest Him.

When Jesus went back to His friends,
He saw they had fallen asleep while He was
praying. Jesus felt sad and lonely.

Suddenly, there were torches in the darkness. Judas stepped out of the darkness. He greeted Jesus, so the soldiers knew which man was Jesus. The soldiers arrested Jesus and marched Him away.

# Three crosses on a hillside

(Matthew 27:31–54)

Everyone who knew Jesus was shocked at what happened next.
Jesus was taken for questioning. No one really knew what
He was there for. They knew He had done nothing wrong.
But His enemies wanted Him out of the way.

Then Jesus, who had healed people, helped them, been kind to them, and forgiven them, was crucified on a hillside between two thieves.

Jesus asked God, His Father, to forgive the soldiers and the thieves and everyone in the world for everything they'd ever done wrong. Jesus was dying for them all.

Then there was an earthquake and darkness in the middle of the day. Jesus took His last breath and died.

# A sad garden
(Luke 23:50–56)

A kind man named Joseph carried Jesus' dead body to his own beautiful garden. Nicodemus helped Joseph.

They buried Jesus in a quiet, dark cave. Then they rolled a big, heavy stone across the opening.

No one could get in. No one could get out.

Jesus' mother was very sad. Jesus' friend John was very sad. They looked after each other. All Jesus' friends were very sad. They knew they would never see Jesus again.

It was the saddest day there had ever been. This day is called Good Friday.

# A happy garden
(Luke 24:1–12; John 20:1–18)

Early on Sunday morning, the women took sweet-
smelling spices to the garden where Jesus was buried.
But they found that the big, heavy stone had been
rolled away. The tomb was empty!

Two shining angels sat beside the grave. "Jesus isn't here," said an angel. "Be happy! Go and tell everyone that He is alive again!"

The women ran to tell Peter and Jesus' other friends, but they could not understand what had happened.

Peter and John ran to the garden and saw the empty tomb for themselves, but they could not understand what had happened.

Mary Magdalene stayed by the empty cave, crying. She could not understand what had happened.

"Mary!" said a kind voice behind her. Mary turned. She knew that voice. It was Jesus! She was so, so happy.

Mary ran back to Peter and Jesus' other friends and told them, "Jesus is alive! I have seen Him!"

It was the happiest day there had ever been!

This day is called Easter.

# Jesus meets two more friends

(Luke 24:13–35)

That very same evening, a man called Cleopas and his friend were walking to a nearby village. They talked together sadly because Jesus had died.

A stranger joined them.

"Why are you so sad?" asked the stranger.

"Haven't You heard?" they answered. "We're sad because Jesus has been crucified. He died on Friday."

Then the man walked with them. He talked, and they listened. He told them wonderful, important things about God.

"Come and have supper with us," said the friends when they reached home. "It's getting dark."

The stranger went into their house and broke some bread, and suddenly the friends knew who He was. The stranger who had walked with them was Jesus!

# Jesus and Thomas
## (John 20)

Jesus was alive again!

"I can't believe it," said Thomas. "I won't believe it unless I see Jesus myself."

Jesus had come to see His disciples on Sunday evening when they were together in a locked room. He had even stayed for supper. But Thomas had not been there. He had missed Jesus.

"But it's true," said Thomas's friends. "We've seen Him. We've spoken to Him. Jesus really is alive!"

A week later, Jesus came to see His friends again. This time, Thomas was there.

"Peace be with you," said Jesus. Then He turned to Thomas. "Look at Me," Jesus said. "Touch Me. Now do you believe I am real, that I am alive?"

Thomas knew that it was Jesus.

"Jesus!" gasped Thomas. "It really is You! You are my Lord and my God."

# Breakfast by the lake
### (John 21)

One night, Peter and his friends were out in their boat, fishing on the lake. They fished and fished and fished all night, but they caught no fish at all.

Just as the sun was rising, they heard a man's voice from the water's edge.

"Have you caught anything?" called the man.

"No, nothing," they replied gloomily. "Not even the tiniest, teeniest fish."

"Put out your net on the right side of the boat," the man shouted back.

So the friends put out their net on the other side of the boat. Then the net was full of so many fish that they could hardly pull it in!

"It's Jesus!" they said.

Peter jumped into the water and waded to the beach. And there was Jesus, making breakfast for them.

The other friends came in the boat, dragging the net full of wiggling, wriggling fish.

"Come and eat," said Jesus, and they all ate fish and bread together on the beach.

# Jesus goes back to heaven

(Acts 1:6–11)

Jesus and His special friends, the disciples, stood on a
hillside and talked to one another.

"Will everyone soon know You are our real
King?" His friends asked Jesus.

"Not quite yet, but one day they will," Jesus said. "I'm going back to heaven soon. I'm going back to My Father. But I want you to tell other people that the way of getting to heaven is to love God and believe that I am the Savior. I will always be with you to help you."

As Jesus spoke, a cloud came down from the sky. When the cloud moved away, Jesus had gone.

As His friends stared up at the sky, two angels stood beside them.

"Don't worry. One day, Jesus will come back," they said.

This day is called Ascension.

121

# Wind and fire

(Acts 2:1–41)

It was a feast day, the festival called Pentecost. Jesus' special friends were all together.

Suddenly, there was a strong wind, a strong and mighty rushing wind that filled the whole house. And the people were amazed to see little flames above Jesus' friends' heads. These were bright flames that didn't burn their hair.

Everyone felt excited and happy. "I want to tell God how much I love Him!" said one.

"I know that God loves me!" said another.

Then they realized they could speak different languages. Jesus made this happen so they could tell other people about Him in their own language. That way all people could

understand that Jesus loves them and forgives their sins.

A big crowd of people from many different countries gathered outside the house.

"What's going on?" the people asked.

Peter talked with them. He told them about Jesus, who was God's Son, come to save them. "God's Spirit has come," Peter said. "It's as if Jesus Himself were here with us, helping us in all we do."

Three thousand people were baptized that day! This day is called Pentecost.

# The Holy Spirit helps
(Acts 3)

God helped Peter and John and Jesus' other disciples to be bold and to know what to say about Him.

Peter spoke to all the crowds of people.

"Jesus is God's Son," said Peter. "He loves you and died for you. He is Lord of all the world. He is King of the whole earth. Stop doing bad things. Tell Him you are sorry. He will forgive you."

Many people listened to Peter. They learned about God together. They prayed to God and praised Him together.

They had meals together. They cared and shared together.

God helped them heal people who were ill, just as Jesus had done. Jesus' friends weren't afraid anymore. They knew that God was always with them, although He was invisible, like the wind.

# Saul's new name

(Acts 9)

A man called Saul loved God, but he hated the Christians.

"I disagree with you," he said. "Stop telling people about Jesus!"

He was so sure he was right that he helped put the Christians in prison. He planned to go to a city called Damascus to stop people from following Jesus. But on the way, something amazing happened. Saul met Jesus!

Saul was surrounded by a light so bright that he couldn't see. He fell to the ground. Then Saul heard a voice.

"Why are you hurting My friends, Saul?" said Jesus. "When you're cruel to the people who love Me, you're being cruel to Me too."

Now Saul knew that Jesus was truly God's Son. Saul wanted Jesus to be his Friend too. Saul joined the Christians and started to tell everyone about Jesus. Now they called him Paul.

Paul was just as happy to help the Christians as he once had been to stop them. News spread everywhere about God's love and forgiveness, and soon people in many places were baptized.

# Peter goes to prison

(Acts 12)

Peter told everyone how much God loved them. He told them that Jesus had died for the sins of the world, but now Jesus was alive again. Everyone could be God's friend and believe in Him.

But some people didn't like what Peter said. They put him in prison and chained him up.

"Let's pray for Peter," said Peter's friends. Together, in Mary's house, they prayed.

Peter was sleeping in the prison when God answered their prayers. He sent an angel to him.

"Wake up!" said the angel. "Follow me."

The chains fell from Peter's wrists. He followed the angel out of the prison.

The prison guards didn't stop him and the big iron gates
swung open for him.

Peter went straight to Mary's house and knocked on the
door. A girl called Rhoda answered.

"It's Peter! It's Peter!" she shouted. She was so excited,
she forgot to let him in!

Peter knocked again. This time, everyone rushed to the
door. Then they thanked God for answering their prayers.

# Paul is shipwrecked!
(Acts 27)

Paul and his friends went to many places to tell people
about Jesus. Sometimes, their journeys were dangerous.
Sometimes, Paul was put in prison.

"I want to go to Rome to see the emperor," said
Paul. "He can decide whether I can go on telling people
about Jesus."

So Paul and his friends sailed to Rome. On the way,
there was a storm. The boat rocked up and down in the big
waves. The boat almost sank in the sea! But God took care of
Paul and his friends.

"God will keep us safe. We won't drown," said Paul. And
they didn't drown.

At last, the boat came to land near the island of Malta.
People there welcomed the sailors and looked after them
until it was safe for them to sail again to Rome.

Paul told the people in Malta about Jesus. When he
arrived in Rome, he was allowed to stay in a house and write
to all his friends. Paul's letters taught people about Jesus and
all He does for us.

# Paul writes thank-you letters

(1 Thessalonians 1; Romans 1)

Paul wrote letters to Christians in some of the places he had visited.

He wrote to tell them that he often thought about them and asked God to look after them.

He wrote to thank them for making him welcome.

He wrote to tell them that God loves them so much that He had sent Jesus to help them.

He wrote to remind them that all people—even Paul himself—need God's forgiveness for their sins. No one is perfect.

He wrote to remind them to love God every day.

And he wrote to remind them to be kind to one another and to share what they had with other people.

# No more tears
(Revelation 4; 21–22)

After Jesus had risen from the grave on Easter, His friend John was sent to live on an island called Patmos. While John was there, he wrote to the people in the Christian churches too.

"God is pure, and God is holy.

"God is good, and God is true and fair.

"Holy, holy, holy is the Lord God Almighty.

"He will live and reign forever.

"All the angels and every creature will worship Him forever and ever."

Then John heard loud trumpets in the starry skies.

He saw a sparkling, flowing river and tree-lined streets. He imagined a wonderful city shining like the sun.

This was a holy city, where no one would be hurt again. There would be no more pain. No one would cry, and no one would ever die again. It was a wonderful place, where everyone who lived there could see God living among them. And they would live forever. (This place is called heaven.)

"Lord Jesus, come and be with everyone," said John.

# Mealtime Prayers

God is great, and God is good,
And we thank Him for our food.
By His hand we all are fed;
Give us, Lord, our daily bread. Amen.

For food and all Your gifts of love,
We give You thanks and praise.
Look down, O Jesus, from above,
And bless us all our days. Amen.

Our hands we fold, our heads we bow;
For food and drink we thank Thee now.

Lord God, heavenly Father, bless us and these
Thy gifts, which we receive from Thy bountiful
goodness, through Jesus Christ, our Lord. Amen.

Grant us Your grace, O Lord, that whatever we eat
or drink and whatever we do, we may do it all in
Your name and to Your glory. Amen.

Come, Lord Jesus, be our Guest,
And let Thy gifts to us be blessed.

# Bedtime Prayers

Now I lay me down to sleep
I pray Thee, Lord, my soul to keep.
Bless and keep me safe this night
And wake me with the morning light.

The day is done; O God the Son,
Look down upon Your little one!
O God of light, keep me this night,
And send to me Your angels bright.
I need not fear since You are near;
You are my Savior, kind and dear. Amen.

Dear Lord God, I pray Thee, for Jesus'
sake, forgive whatever I have done wrong
today, and keep me safe this night. Amen.

Be near me, Lord Jesus,
I ask You to stay
Close by me forever
And love me, I pray.
Bless all the dear children
In Your tender care
And take us to heaven to live with You there.

I thank You, my heavenly Father, through
Jesus Christ, Your dear Son, that You have
graciously kept me this day; and I pray that
You would forgive me all my sins where I have
done wrong, and graciously keep me this
night. For into Your hands I commend
myself, my body and soul, and all things.
Let Your holy angel be with me, that
the evil foe may have no power over me.
Amen.

*Luther's Evening Prayer*

# The Lord's Prayer

Our Father who art in heaven,
hallowed be Thy name,
Thy kingdom come,
Thy will be done on earth
as it is in heaven;
give us this day our daily bread;
and forgive us our trespasses
as we forgive those
who trespass against us;
and lead us not into temptation,
but deliver us from evil.
For Thine is the kingdom
and the power and the glory
forever and ever. Amen.

# Blessing

The LORD bless you and keep you;
the LORD make His face to shine upon you
and be gracious to you;
the LORD lift up His countenance upon you
and give you peace.

*Numbers 6:24–26*

⚓ This edition published 2015 by Concordia Publishing House

Copyright © 2012 Anno Domini Publishing
Book House, Orchard Mews, 18 High Street, Tring,
Herts, HP23 5AH England
www.ad-publishing.com
Text copyright © 2012 Lizzie Ribbons
Illustrations copyright © 2012 Paola Bertolini Grudina

Publishing Director: Annette Reynolds
Art Director: Gerald Rogers
Pre-production Manager: Doug Hewitt
All rights reserved

Printed and bound in Malaysia / 00920 / 410674